Teen Issues

BULLYING

Lori Hile

Heinemann
LIBRARY

Chicago, Illinois

www.capstonepub.com
Visit our website to find out more information about Heinemann-Raintree books.

To order:

☎ Phone 800-747-4992

🖳 Visit www.capstonepub.com
to browse our catalog and order online.

Edited by Andrew Farrow, Adam Miller, and
 Vaarunika Dharmapala
Designed by Steve Mead and Clare Webber

Originated by Capstone Global Library Ltd
Printed and bound in the United States of America in North Mankato, Minnesota. 112012 007019RP

16 15 14 13
10 9 8 7 6 5 4 3 2

Library of Congress Cataloging-in-Publication Data
Hile, Lori.

 Bullying / Lori Hile.

  p. cm.—(Teen issues)

 Includes bibliographical references and index.

 ISBN 978-1-4329-6534-1 (hb)—ISBN 978-1-4329-6539-6 (pb) 1. Bullying. 2. Bullying—Prevention. 3. Cyberbullying. I. Title.

 BF637.B85H55 2013

 302.34'3—dc23   2011039225

Acknowledgments
We would like to thank the following for permission to reproduce photographs: Alamy pp. 7 (© Chris Rout), 20 (© Richard Levine), 25 (© Bubbles Photolibrary), 26 (© fotovisage), 41 (© UpperCut Images), 44 (© Anne-Marie Palmer); Corbis p. 32 (© Weston Colton/Rubberball); Getty Images pp. 14, 29 (Image Source), 18 (Yellow Dog Productions/The Image Bank), 31 (Steve Liss/Time & Life Pictures), 35 (Matt Cardy), 36 (Alberto E. Rodriguez); Glow Images p. 23 (Stockbroker); © Newspix/News Ltd/3rd Party Managed Reproduction & Supply Rights/Sam Ruttyn p. 49; Photolibrary p. 11 (John Carey), 38 (KPA KPA); Press Association Images p. 4 (AP Photo/The Republican, Don Treeger); QMI Agency p. 17; Science Photo Library p. 12 (Wellcome Dept of Imaging Neuroscience); Superstock p. 47 (© Ambient Images Inc.).

Cover photograph of four girls reproduced with permission of Photolibrary (Stockbroker).

In order to protect the privacy of individuals featured in this book, some names may have been changed.

Every effort has been made to contact copyright holders of any material reproduced in this book. Any omissions will be rectified in subsequent printings if notice is given to the publisher.

Disclaimer
All the Internet addresses (URLs) given in this book were valid at the time of going to press. However, due to the dynamic nature of the Internet, some addresses may have changed, or sites may have changed or ceased to exist since publication. While the author and publisher regret any inconvenience this may cause readers, no responsibility for any such changes can be accepted by either the author or the publisher.

CONTENTS

Some words are shown in bold, **like this**. You can find out what they mean by looking in the glossary.

STORIES OF BULLYING

This candlelight vigil is being held to honor Phoebe Prince, who committed suicide after enduring months of bullying.

REAL-LIFE TRAGEDIES

- When 15-year-old Phoebe Prince moved from Ireland to a small town in Massachusetts in 2009, she quickly captured the attention of the boys at school. She went out with Todd Mulveyhil, captain of the football team, which angered Todd's ex-girlfriend. She and her friends began calling Phoebe names. They knocked books out of her hands and shoved her into lockers. They bombarded her with threatening phone messages and Facebook posts, some even encouraging Phoebe to kill herself. On January 14, 2010, Phoebe walked home from school and hanged herself.

- In 2010, a group of boys wearing school uniforms led another boy across a schoolyard and struck him in the head. The boy fell to the ground, where he lay crumpled. The boys filmed the incident and posted it on a video-sharing site.

- In 2011, Emily Nakanda, 15, cracked her knuckles before grabbing her classmate Anna by the hair and putting her in a headlock. Then she threatened to tear out Anna's hair. She also punched Anna and shoved her to the ground. In case anyone missed the incident, which took place in a London alley, Emily's friends filmed it on a cell phone and forwarded footage to their **peers**.

These true stories showcase some of the tragic consequences of bullying. While these incidents made headlines and shocked many people, the truth is that bullying occurs every day in playgrounds, classrooms, and on computers around the globe. Fortunately, most incidences of bullying are less extreme, and many people are stepping up efforts to prevent bullying in the first place.

Changing attitudes

Of course, bullying is nothing new. The chances are your parents were bullied at some point or knew people who were. However, a few things have changed in recent years. For one thing, bullies can now follow their **targets** around not just at school, but also online and on cell phones. Insults can be broadcast instantly for the entire school—or Internet—to see. Bullies can also cause more destruction, since weapons have become more widespread and violence has become more common.

Tragedies like the ones described on page 5 have helped alert many adults to the severity of bullying. In the past, bullying was sometimes seen as a normal rite of passage—as "kids being kids." Bullied kids were sometimes told to "toughen up." Many of them kept quiet, partly because they felt ashamed.

Now, armed with new information about the harmful effects of bullying, many people are beginning to see bullying as behavior no more acceptable than child abuse. If parents beat their children or threaten them, the police can be called. Why should it be any different if it is a child making the threats or throwing the punches? Their actions harm their victims just as much, if not more. People are beginning to realize that it is bullies who should feel ashamed, not their victims.

Breaking the bullying cycle

Changing attitudes and actions is never easy. Bullying is often a cycle, since bullies have often been bullied themselves by parents or other people. In order to stop bullying, educators, parents, communities, and young people all need to work together. This book will help you to better understand bullying, so that you can do your part.

TRUE OR FALSE?

Bullying is normal.

False. Bullying may be common, just like child abuse and **domestic abuse**. That does not mean, however, that it is normal or acceptable. Bullying is **antisocial** behavior that should not be tolerated.

Bullying beyond the playground

Bullying peaks in middle school, then tapers off in high school. However, that does not stop some adults from bullying, at home and in the workplace. One in six employees experiences bullying at work, which makes it more common than **sexual harassment**. Workplace bullies often spread damaging or false rumors about their coworkers or criticize them in front of important people. These actions can increase employee stress and illness and make for a miserable work environment. Many deserving employees also lose the opportunity for advancement if they have been bad-mouthed by a bully. Unfortunately, there are few laws against this type of behavior, and most companies have no rules against it. The good news is that learning how to combat bullies now will make it much easier to handle workplace bullies later in life.

TYPES OF BULLYING

Normal conflict	Bullying behavior
Young people have a disagreement with each other.	The attack usually comes out of nowhere. The bully may try to justify his or her behavior by blaming the victim, but the victim has done nothing to provoke the bully.
Both kids may experience feelings of anger or frustration.	Both kids experience very different feelings. Only one of them (the victim) feels hurt or upset. The other (the bully) sometimes gets pleasure from abusing the victim.
When one child shouts, the other child feels comfortable standing up for himself or herself.	Only the bully is allowed to shout. If the victim expresses hurt or anger, the bully may mock the victim or express indifference.
Young people may take turns starting an argument, and disagreements happen only occasionally.	The bully always starts the "fight" and abuses the victim repeatedly.
Young people may find it possible to resolve the issue through discussion.	The conflict is impossible to resolve, because there is no real conflict.

Bullying versus normal conflict

Everyone has disagreements. Some conflicts can even be healthy, because they can help you learn how to resolve problems. However, it is important not to mistake bullying for normal, acceptable conflict.

So, what exactly is bullying? Is it punching or shoving someone? **Taunting** or name-calling? What about excluding another person from a group? Making racist remarks? Bullying can take any of these forms. It is most commonly defined as any ongoing physical, social, or verbal abuse that is intended to harm the victim (often called a "target"), who is less powerful in some way.

There are three main elements that make bullying "bullying":

1 *An imbalance of power between the bully and the target*: The child who bullies may be stronger than his or her victim, or better at flinging insults or threats. The bully may also be more confident than the target and have more friends, or more popular friends, to back him or her up. This is called "social power."

2 *Intent to harm*: A bully does not accidentally step on your toe and then say sorry. A bully stomps on your foot in a deliberate attempt to hurt or upset you. The bully may apologize, but the apology is insincere.

3 *Ongoing aggression*: Bullying is rarely a single occurrence. Usually the bully repeats his or her behavior, often in the same places, as a way to establish dominance. Many of these spots lack adult supervision, which allows kids to bully without getting caught. Bullies often threaten to make the target's life miserable if he or she ever tells an adult.

However, a single incident can count as bullying, too. One eight-year-old girl was chased around her friend's backyard by her friend and another girl, who were both bigger and more popular. For hours, they taunted and followed her. When the girl tried to alert her friend's father, the "friend" insisted that her father was asleep and would be angry if the girl knocked on the door. Although it was a one-time occurrence, the girl went home sobbing and still remembers the incident years later.

Direct and indirect bullying

When people think of bullying, they often picture a big child punching a smaller child in the face. This is a form of **direct bullying**, in which bullies use words or force to abuse someone face-to-face. Bullying can also happen indirectly—behind someone's back—with passed notes, whispered rumors, or Internet threats.

Direct bullying: Physical

Sixteen-year-old Kevin was editor of his school newspaper and captain of the swimming team. As he stood at his locker to pull on his team jacket, he felt something hit his neck. He whirled around to see four boys: two standing guard and two throwing rocks at his head. Seconds later, Kevin collapsed, and the boys ran off with his jacket, but not before kicking him. Kevin was found **unconscious** and rushed to the hospital, where he lay **paralyzed** for days. Fortunately, Kevin's paralysis was temporary, and he made a full recovery.

Kevin's story is an instance of **physical bullying**. Although physical attacks and their consequences are the most visible form of bullying, less than one-third of all bullying is physical.

Physical attacks have become increasingly violent over the past 20 years. As access to guns and knives has grown in the Western world, so have violent attacks among teenagers, including murder. Of course, teenagers can inflict severe physical harm even without weapons. In some cases, teenagers have kicked and beaten both children and adults, while filming the incidents and posting them on the Internet. In several cases, the victims have died of injuries from the attacks.

Other examples of physical bullying include:

- blocking access to hallways or bathrooms
- "pantsing" (sneaking up behind someone and pulling his or her pants down)
- breaking or stealing personal belongings.

Both boys and girls engage in physical bullying, although girls are more likely to engage in **verbal bullying** (see the next page).

Some bullies forward violent videos like this on to others.

Direct bullying: Verbal

Ruby, age 12, takes one look at Chloe's new outfit and says to her friends, "Look at Chloe's 'little girl' dress. What is she, six years old?" Ruby's friends laugh, but Chloe casts her eyes down and walks away.

Whoever wrote the childhood chant, "Sticks and stones will break my bones, but names will never hurt me" was clearly never mocked by a teenage bully. Physical bullying may receive more attention, but a majority of teenagers describe verbal bullying—that is, using words to taunt, threaten, or mock—as more painful. It is also more common, accounting for up to 70 percent of reported bullying.

Adolescents can be especially damaged by verbal bullying, because they are often trying to figure out just who they are. Instead of looking to parents, most teenagers turn to their peers for feedback about their strengths and weaknesses. If teenagers are mocked or insulted by bullies, they may start to lose confidence in their abilities.

Examples of verbal bullying include:

- swearing or threats
- name-calling or taunting
- mocking or imitating
- laughing at someone's mistakes
- consistently disagreeing with someone's point of view.

Teasing or taunting?

Lots of people claim they are "just joking" after saying something hurtful, but there is nothing funny about saying cruel or unkind things. **Teasing** is OK; taunting is not. Here are some differences between the two:

Teasing	Taunting
The teaser and the person being teased can swap roles.	One person does all the taunting.
It is meant to make both people laugh.	It is meant to make the target feel bad.
It pokes fun in a playful way.	Remarks are cruel or humiliating.
It is a small part of a relationship.	It is a large part of a relationship.
It stops when the person being teased objects.	It continues even after the person being taunted becomes upset.

Other forms of direct bullying include:

- *Sexual bullying*: Sexual bullying is any abusive behavior that is based on a person's gender or sexuality, or sexual orientation. It can include unwanted touching or spreading rumors about a person's sex life or orientation.

- *Hazing*: To join a sports team, some students are forced to participate in humiliating or dangerous activities.

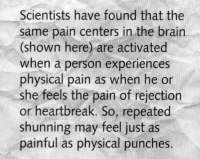

Scientists have found that the same pain centers in the brain (shown here) are activated when a person experiences physical pain as when he or she feels the pain of rejection or heartbreak. So, repeated shunning may feel just as painful as physical punches.

THE SILENT TREATMENT:
LUCY, CATHERINE, AND JACKIE

Lucy had been best friends with Catherine and Jackie since they were in preschool together. When they began middle school, Catherine and Jackie joined in with a bigger group of girls. Lucy joined them, but never felt completely accepted by the group's "leaders." One day, when Lucy sat down at the group's lunch table, all the other girls acted like she was not even there. Lucy ate her lunch in painful silence, wondering what she did wrong.

Indirect bullying

Lucy's story is an example of what is sometimes called **relational aggression**, a form of **indirect bullying** that intentionally damages someone's relationships, **self-esteem**, or acceptance within a group. A bully may, for instance, tell other kids to stop being friends with someone or encourage them to give that person the "silent treatment."

Both girls and boys are guilty of relational bullying, but girls engage in it differently and more frequently. When a group of boys decides to exclude someone, they usually pick an individual from outside their circle of friends. Girls may suddenly decide to exclude a girl from within their own group, which can leave their victim feeling deeply hurt and confused. A betrayal by "friends" is usually more painful than rejection from strangers. Since teenage girls often place a great deal of value on relationships, rejection can leave them feeling particularly isolated or worthless.

Relational bullying is the least noticeable form of bullying, but it can be extremely harmful to both girls and boys. One study found that girls who experienced frequent, indirect bullying were nine times more likely to be depressed and three times more likely to think about suicide than average. Boys who regularly experienced indirect bullying were eleven times more likely to be depressed and five times more likely to consider suicide than average.

RICKY AND OLIVIA: CYBERBULLYING

Ricky Alatorre, a heavyset 16-year-old living in a small Indiana farm town, was minding his own business when a classmate secretly snapped his photo during English class. Soon afterward, a fake profile turned up on MySpace, mocking Ricky's weight and grades and claiming that Ricky was gay (he is not). "I was completely devastated," Ricky says. "When you put it on the Internet, you are opening it up to everyone in the world." MySpace removed the fake page, but not for several weeks. In the meantime, Ricky—who had never had a lot of friends—felt more alone than ever. He even considered suicide. Fortunately, with the support of his parents and school officials—who started an anti-bullying program—Ricky is still in school.

Olivia Gardner was bullied in elementary school, after suffering an **epileptic** seizure in front of her classmates. It began with name-calling and taunting in the hallways. Then her peers started an "Olivia Haters" web site. In school, her classmates wore "I Hate Olivia" bracelets. Olivia thought about suicide and might have followed through, if two sisters, Emily and Sarah, had not read Olivia's story in a local newspaper. They asked their friends to write Olivia letters of encouragement. Soon, thousands of letters poured in from around the world. Olivia, who had left school, is now back. She will never forget the pain caused by her bullies, but she has hope for the future.

Victims of cyberbullying cannot escape bullies even in the safety of their own bedrooms.

What is cyberbullying?

Ricky and Olivia were victims of **cyberbullying**, which is the use of communications technologies such as the Internet, computers, or cell phones to **harass**, humiliate, or threaten another person. Between 2005 and 2010, cyberbullying increased by 100 percent, to become the most common **medium** for bullying.

Young people can escape most types of bullying once they enter their own homes, but cyberbullying does not stop at the front door. Cyberbullies can "follow" their victims anywhere. This constant stress can lead to physical symptoms such as mood swings, changes in appetite, and sleep problems.

Cyberbullies may hide behind fake screen names or profiles. This **anonymity** allows them to say more vicious things than they might say face-to-face. Despite this, 75 percent of teenagers say they know the identity of their cyberbully, and most cyberbullies can be tracked.

Forms of cyberbullying

Some of the most common forms of cyberbullying include:

- *Posting humiliating photos*: Bullies may secretly take unflattering photos of classmates or "Photoshop" classmates' pictures on to other people's bodies.
- *Cell phone pranks*: Bullies may write a victim's phone number on the bathroom wall.
- *Cyberstalking*: Cyberstalkers closely follow someone's online activity and send threatening or unwanted messages.
- *Exclusion*: Teenagers may block others from joining an Instant Messaging group or from seeing an online event invitation.
- *Impersonation*: Bullies may create a fake social network page for another person, or steal someone's password and invade his or her e-mail or social network.
- *Online slam books*: Students contribute unkind comments about a particular classmate on an online "notebook," before forwarding it to the target.
- *Text wars*: Bullies may bombard a victim with hundreds of abusive text messages.

Dealing with cyberbullying

Here is how you can reduce your chances of becoming a victim of cyberbullying:

- *Be respectful*: Studies show that gossiping about or bad-mouthing others may increase your risk of being bullied.

- *Protect yourself online*: Only open messages from people you know, and think carefully before sharing personal information and photos.

- *Protect your password*: Password-protect both your cell phone and your online sites, and change the passwords often. Never give your passwords to anyone other than your parents.

Do not BE the bully

When you go online:

- *Pause*: Before you hit "send," take a few seconds to think about how your message or photo might affect another person's feelings.

- *Step up*: If you forward a nasty message or stand by while a bully does so, you are helping to harm an innocent person. Let the bully know that his or her action is cruel, not cool. If you are unable to stop the bully, report him or her and help the victim.

- *Think about the consequences*: Schools can suspend bullies, and cyberbullies can face severe legal trouble.

If you do become a victim of cyberbullying, there are steps you can take to stop the abuse:

- *Tell a trusted adult immediately*: Not only is cyberbullying harmful, it may also be against the rules of your school, or even against the law. A parent can contact your cell phone company, social networking site, or Internet service provider to trace calls, texts, or messages and help block them. An adult can also contact the school or police.

- *Block the bully*: Change the privacy settings on your social networking site so your bully cannot reach you.

- *Save the evidence*: The only good news about cyberbullying is that your bully leaves evidence. Save it! You can forward text messages to a parent's phone or take a screen grab of nasty comments in chat rooms or social networking pages.

- *Resist the urge to retaliate*: Getting back at the bully only turns you into a bully yourself and could start a cyber war. A bully wants you to respond. Do not give him or her that kind of power!

DAVID AND TRAVIS'S STORY: FIGHTING BULLYING WITH TECHNOLOGY

When a teenage boy wore a pink shirt on the first day of school in a small Canadian town, he was harassed by bullies, who called him a "homo" and threatened to beat him up. Two older teenagers, David Shepherd and Travis Price, heard the news and decided to take action. They purchased 50 cheap pink T-shirts, then e-mailed all their classmates, encouraging them to combat bullying by transforming the school into a "sea of pink" the next day. Not only did many students wear the pink T-shirts, but hundreds more came dressed head-to-toe in their own pink clothes. When the bullied child saw all his classmates decked out in pink, Shepherd said, "He went from looking depressed to being as happy as can be. It looked like … a big weight lifted off his shoulders." Since then, the bullies have left the boy alone.

Since David Shepherd and Travis Price came up with the idea, other schools have held annual "sea of pink" events, as a way to protest bullying.

THE BULLY

Bullies may look scary, but many are themselves very unhappy. The majority of bullies have been bullied by parents, siblings, or other young people.

DEAN'S STORY: FAMILY VIOLENCE

Seven-year-old Dean's behavior in class was so bad that he nearly made his teacher quit. Dean constantly talked over his teacher's lessons, shoved other students, and untied their shoelaces. In short, Dean was a bully. A psychologist named Dr. Marty worked with troubled kids in the school. In his blog, Dr. Marty said he realized that Dean had trouble sitting still in class. Dr. Marty let Dean move around his room as he learned.

Despite this help, Dean still got into trouble. After Dean pushed a boy into a mud puddle, Dr. Marty asked Dean to draw pictures of his family. Dean included his mother, his guinea pigs, and his fish. Then he drew another picture, in black, of his mother being thrown against a wall. Then a picture of a man beating his mother up. Dr. Marty learned that Dean had never known his father, and that his mother's boyfriend had hit her and may have hit Dean, too.

Although all bullies are different, many share backgrounds similar to Dean's. Bullies are more likely than other kids to come from single-parent homes, where they may receive less supervision and attention. They are also more likely to witness violent behavior at home, as Dean did. As many as 97 percent of kids who bully say they have been bullied themselves.

Like Dean, many bullies also struggle in school. Because they lack positive reinforcement for their work, they may feel frustrated and seek attention any way they can get it.

Understanding a bully's background and motives will never excuse a bully's behavior or make bullying any less painful, but it can help victims realize that bullies are often weaker than they might think. Bullies are not monsters. Sometimes, they are sad and frightened boys and girls—people to pity, not fear.

TRUE OR FALSE?

People are born bullies.

False. Bullying is a learned behavior. All humans have aggressive tendencies, some more than others. Even so, no one becomes a bully unless they see these behaviors modeled by family or friends. Fortunately, bullying behaviors can also be "unlearned."

Common characteristics of a bully

Bullies come in all shapes and sizes, but one thing they have in common is that they tend to have trouble **empathizing**. Bullies are often good at predicting how their behavior will affect another person, and at reading their victim's responses. However, they cannot easily relate to the other person's pain. Bullies often underestimate the emotional effect their actions have. Since some bullies can brush off a bullying incident without a second thought, they might assume that their victims can, too.

Bullies may have trouble managing anger. They may have learned from their role models that anger is a normal and appropriate response to conflict, or they may have impulse-control problems. This means it is harder for them to control angry outbursts.

They may refuse to take responsibility for their actions. One bully, for instance, shook a ladder on which a maintenance man was working. The man fell down and reported the bully, who was suspended from school. When the bully later saw the worker, he did not apologize. Instead, he angrily told the man, "You got me in trouble!"

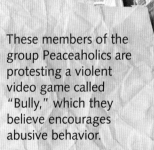

These members of the group Peaceaholics are protesting a violent video game called "Bully," which they believe encourages abusive behavior.

Why do bullies bully?

People bully for many reasons:

- *They need to feel powerful*: Many bullies feel powerless over problems or people at home. Bullying allows them to control or dominate another person.

- *They want to be popular*: Power can bring popularity. What bullies may not know is that most young people actually have a negative view of others who have gained popularity by bullying.

- *They believe others are more aggressive than they are*: Because bullies often have aggressive role models, they tend to assume that everyone is aggressive. Sometimes they interpret innocent actions (such as someone accidentally stepping on their foot) as deliberate and hostile.

- *Because they can*: It sounds simple, but if bullies have the opportunity to hurt someone else for their own gain, they will often take it. If no one questions their bad behavior, they will probably continue and even begin to believe it is acceptable.

- *They envy others*: Bullies often taunt those who have qualities they admire, even if they are not aware of it at the time.

- *They may have a negative view of themselves*: Some bullies have been taught by their parents that they are worthless. They are worried others will see their inadequacy, so they focus on other people's "faults" instead.

- *They may think of themselves as superior to others*: Many bullies have been taught to hate or disrespect people who are different from them, and to target these individuals.

The self-esteem puzzle

For years, experts assumed bullies had low self-esteem and put others down as a way to feel better about themselves. Recent surveys show, however, that many bullies say they like who they are. If this is true, why do bullies put others down? It is possible bullies like themselves partly because they are unaware of what others really think of them. Many kids are afraid of bullies and do not dare tell them the truth. Some bullies may simply not admit to feelings of insecurity or inadequacy.

Bullying by girls

In 2000, scientists conducted an experiment in which girl babies were dressed in blue and boy babies were dressed in pink. Adults praised the "pink" babies as "sweet" and "pretty," assuming they were girls. The "blue" babies, assumed to be boys, were admired as "big" and "strong." This experiment showed that girls and boys are assigned different roles at a very young age. Boys are expected to be strong, independent, and competitive. Girls are expected to be sweet, pretty, and cooperative—not competitive.

Despite social expectations girls, just like boys, are always competing: for good grades, boyfriends, friends, and popularity. Competition results in winners and losers, as well as jealousy and anger. Since girls are discouraged from expressing aggressive feelings, they sometimes do it indirectly. Instead of confronting the object of their jealousy or anger, girls may simply ignore, shun, or spread nasty rumors about the person.

Girls who engage in this type of aggression may seem sweet on the surface, but they can be unkind and **manipulative** underneath. Bullies like these are sometimes called "mean girls." This type of behavior is often seen simply as "normal" or "what girls do," rather than bullying. However, it is actually one of the most harmful forms of bullying, because it can result in the loss or betrayal of friends. If girls can learn to acknowledge their feelings of jealousy, anger, and competition, they can express these feelings in a more open and less destructive way.

A reason for shunning?

In early societies, shunning may have served an important cultural function. Since there were no formal police forces or prisons, communities simply excluded people who engaged in antisocial behavior. However, today, shunning itself is considered antisocial.

Girls, especially in groups, can be just as cruel as boys.

Dealing with girl bullying

Because girl bullying is often indirect, many teachers never notice it. This makes it especially important to bring it to a teacher's attention, so that he or she can address the behavior. It can also pay to talk to the bully yourself. In a calm, confident tone, try telling your bully, "I don't like what you are doing, and I'd like you to stop." If the girl continues to bully, you should refuse to raise your voice while also refusing to back down.

You can also directly address a rumor with a comment such as, "I heard that you called me 'fatty.' Is this true?" If the bully denies it, you can say, "That's good, because I thought we were friends, and a friend would never call me nasty names behind my back."

It can also be helpful to remember that you do not need to please girls who bully you or try to be their friends. They may seem important and powerful now, but it is much more important to hang around people who boost your self-esteem, rather than tear it down.

Why bullies should change

Do bullies ever change their ways? Since bullies sometimes feel a sense of power when they bully, they may not feel an immediate need to change their behavior. In fact, bullies are harming not only their victims, but also themselves. Bullies are more likely to get into trouble at school and with the law. In one study, seven- and eight-year-old children who were identified as bullies were six times more likely than non-bullies to be convicted of at least one crime by the age of 24. Bullies are also far more likely than average to experience problems with relationships, careers, and mental health. In short, bullies have every reason to change—and some do.

Problems for bullies

Healthy relationships require **empathy**. To feel close to others, we must care how our behavior affects them. Bullies can find it hard to experience empathy. In school, bullies may be popular because they seem powerful. As we grow older, however, behavior that used to be cool starts to seem immature. Teenagers who treat others with respect are drawn together, and bullies become people to avoid. The pattern of bad behavior does not stop in school. Bullies are often manipulative, cruel, or abusive with partners and children and end up destroying these relationships, too.

Underneath their swagger, many bullies are depressed. Bullies often hide feelings of shame and sadness, since these make them feel weak. Asking for help makes bullies feel **vulnerable** and powerless. Their depression is rarely detected by others, because it is easier to see someone's bad behavior than it is to identify what is happening inside their head. Left untreated, depression increases the likelihood that bullies will continue their abuse, since bullying may temporarily make them feel better.

Bullies also tend to struggle academically more than other students. Studies show they generally have a more negative attitude about school than non-bullies, which leads them to perform poorly and perhaps to drop out early. Bullies generally have fewer years of education than non-bullies and lower-paying jobs. Overall, those identified early on as bullies are also less satisfied with their careers.

Bullies can change

The good news is that bullies can change, especially if they receive help early. Many bullies are hurt and angry, but instead of sharing these feelings, they take them out on other people. Unless bullies learn to manage their anger, they will continue hurting and alienating others from their lives.

Fortunately, there are other feelings, such as annoyance or frustration, that come before anger. So, when a person first feels a hint of irritation, he or she can stop and think: "What will happen if I lose my temper?" and "What will happen if I stay calm?" No one is perfect, but with practice, it is possible to get anger under control.

Kids identified as bullies in school have been found to be more likely than non-bullies to commit a serious crime in adulthood.

TARGETS OF BULLYING

Although bullies often target those who are a bit different, those unique qualities can serve victims well in the future.

"Children are bullied for thousands of reasons, none of them valid."

Bullying expert
Barbara Coloroso

Why are some young people frequently targeted by bullies? The truth is most bullies do not care who their victim is, as long as it is someone they believe they can **intimidate**. The target is usually different from their peers in some way. Bullies use that difference as an excuse to bully and as a way to get others on their side.

Common targets

Interviews were done with young people between the ages of 12 and 16 who had been identified by their teachers as bullies. In these interviews, the bullies admitted that they often targeted those who performed poorly in sports or in school. They also said they most frequently picked on students believed to be gay or lesbian. Surveys support this. Over 90 percent of gay and lesbian students between the ages of 13 to 18 have been bullied or harassed at least once. They are also more likely to commit suicide than other students.

Other common targets include:
- young people with disabilities
- very overweight or very skinny kids
- young people with noticeable physical differences—for example, big ears, braces, glasses, or acne
- new students
- young people of a different race, religion, or ethnicity from the bully or from the majority of students
- highly intelligent students.

Even more important than physical traits are emotional ones, such as:
- *Shy kids*: Young people who are **passive** and shy may not know how to defend themselves against more aggressive peers and may be more sensitive to attacks from bullies.
- *Loners*: Young people who keep to themselves are often targeted, mainly because they do not have a lot of friends to back them up.

Something special

On a positive note, targets of bullying are often smarter, more sensitive, and more imaginative than other kids. Many bullying victims grow up to become successful adults.

Effects of bullying on targets

Have you ever felt a knot in the pit of your stomach before an important test or speech? Imagine walking around with a knot in your stomach all day, every day. This is how many victims of bullying feel. When threatened, our brains trigger what is commonly called a fight-or-flight response. Our heart rate increases and our senses are sharpened. This can be useful if you need to escape something dangerous, such as a bear attack, but it is not healthy on an ongoing basis. Living in a constant state of fear or stress can produce symptoms such as headaches and stomachaches, skin disorders, nightmares, nervous tics, and the kind of **traumatic** stress disorders sometimes experienced by soldiers in war.

Bullying can also lead to emotional problems. Teenagers who are repeatedly bullied about their weight develop **anorexia**, **bulimia**, and other eating disorders at higher rates than average. In one survey, over 90 percent of people suffering from eating disorders said they had been bullied. Half of them believed that bullying directly triggered their disorder.

Many bullied teenagers also develop substance abuse problems. Some use drugs or alcohol to look cool among their peers or to temporarily relieve the pain of being bullied. However, the younger a child is when he or she first uses alcohol or drugs, the greater the chance he or she has of becoming addicted.

Education

Over 160,000 kids in the United States miss school each day to avoid attacks or threats, and 10 percent drop out of high school entirely. Even bullied students who attend school regularly can have trouble learning. When a student is bullied, the **amygdala**, or "fight-or-flight" area of the brain, is activated. Unfortunately, this prevents the **frontal lobe**, or "thinking area" of the brain, from being engaged. Without the ability to think clearly, it is almost impossible for victims of bullying to focus on classes. People cannot learn when they are afraid. Even so, many bullied teenagers are highly intelligent and see learning as an escape from bullying. They perform well despite the bullying and later make valuable contributions to society.

You can prevent violence

If you or anyone you know is considering using violence against themselves or anyone else, immediately contact a trusted adult or emergency hotline.

Low self-esteem and depression

Often teenagers with low self-esteem are targeted by bullies, and bullying only makes the problem worse. When placed in a new environment, these victims may expect that others will automatically abuse or reject them. Worse yet, many believe that they somehow deserve it. This low self-confidence can prevent them from finding new friends or pursuing new activities.

Victims of bullying often suffer from depression. In fact, victims of all the various kinds of bullying are about four times more likely than non-victims to suffer from severe depression, insomnia (difficulty sleeping), and anxiety.

Kids who are constantly threatened by bullies are often more focused on their survival than their studies.

BRIAN'S STORY: BULLIED TO DEATH

Brian Head, a 15-year-old from Georgia, was described as a quiet, caring boy and a talented poet. He was also a constant target for bullies. They would break his glasses, bloody his nose, slam him into lockers, and taunt him for being chubby. His mother mistakenly believed it was "normal kid stuff."

On March 28, 1994, Brian walked into his class and shouted, "I can't take it anymore!" Then he pulled out a gun and shot himself in the head.

Lifelong scars: The effects of bullying

Bullying victims who are sad or angry sometimes direct those feelings toward themselves and others. Unfortunately, tragic stories such as Brian's are becoming increasingly common. Bullying has been linked to so many teenage suicides that there is now a word for the phenomenon: "bullycide." In the United States, the number of teen suicide attempts tripled between 1990 and 2003, although it is difficult to determine how many of them were linked to bullying.

Given the opportunity, some victims of bullying become bullies themselves. Tired of feeling helpless, they target those they can feel powerful around. For instance, a child who is verbally abused by her mother might verbally abuse her classmates.

Some bullying victims fantasize about taking revenge on their bullies. Out of 37 recent school shootings, more than two-thirds of the attackers said they had felt bullied by other kids prior to the shooting. This type of violent revenge may give the students a temporary feeling of power, but it can never justify the horrific damage they cause, nor undo the painful effects of being bullied.

The majority of bullied kids do not hurt anyone else or engage in bullying behavior. Many young people who are bullied do, however, begin to believe the negative messages they receive from their bullies about themselves. This can cause a lot of harm to them for many years after the bullying has stopped.

It may have become difficult for them to tell the difference between the bully's voice and their own. The actual bully is no longer necessary, because the bully now lives inside the victim's head. Even when their real-life accomplishments contradict the bully's message, former victims may have a hard time believing in their own worth.

Long-term effects

The scars of bullying can last into adulthood. Adults may not remember all the math they learned in school, but they almost certainly remember the names and faces of their childhood bullies, as well as their harmful words or actions. Those painful memories can make it difficult for former bullying victims to trust or let others become close to them. They may have a lingering fear or expectation that they will be betrayed or abused by the people in their lives. To avoid that pain, they may keep others at a distance. Also, if former victims have never learned how to be **assertive**, they may continue to be bullied, at work or in other relationships. Some former victims are even drawn to bullies, perhaps as a second chance to stand up to their childhood abusers.

This is a memorial to the victims of the Columbine High School massacre in Colorado. Dylan Klebold, a victim of bullying, and his friend Eric Harris killed 13 people and wounded another 23. They then both killed themselves.

THE BYSTANDER

Many young people who witness bullying may not help the victim because they believe their own popularity depends on siding with a bully.

In the school cafeteria, seven-year-old Evie deliberately poured a drink on Hannah's pants. Hannah was upset, but Evie was not finished yet. When Hannah stood up to leave, Evie announced to the whole cafeteria, "Look at Hannah! She wet herself." Everyone laughed. Now, Hannah was devastated and Evie was satisfied.

The children who laughed probably did not realize that they were helping the bully. Without their laughter, however, the bully would not have fully succeeded in humiliating the other girl. Bullies love an audience. It gives them the attention they crave and helps them feel more powerful and less guilty about their actions. It should be no surprise, then, that 85 percent of bullying incidents take place in a group setting.

The kids who witness bullying are often called **bystanders**. In many bullying situations, there is usually just one bully and one victim, but there are lots of bystanders. Over 70 percent of kids fall into the bystander category, which gives them a lot of power. In this example, the bystanders used their power to encourage the bully.

Bystanders can also take a more active role, helping the bully play a nasty joke. They can also simply remain silent when they see a bully hurt someone. The good news is that bystanders can also use their power to stand up to the bully and defend the victim.

Roots of Empathy

Can watching a helpless baby increase empathy? In Canada's Roots of Empathy program, a parent and an infant visit the same classroom every three weeks. Students learn about the parent's struggles and learn to identify what the baby might be feeling. This helps students put themselves in other people's shoes, which is at the root of empathy.

Why don't bystanders intervene?

When bystanders do intervene in bullying, they can usually stop the bully about half of the time. Unfortunately, some observers say that bystanders only intervene in about 13 percent of bullying incidents. Why is this?

- *Fear*: Some people are afraid of getting hurt themselves. If the bully is bigger or stronger, it is sensible to find an adult to help. Other people are afraid of becoming a new target for the bully. Still others are afraid they will just make the bully angrier and the situation worse.

- *Ignorance*: Some bystanders might want to help, but simply do not know what to do.

- *Indifference*: Young people who witness bullying may say: "It's not my problem" or, "It's not my friend," then turn away. They may not directly contribute to the bullying, but the action of turning away is still an action, and one that can leave a victim in danger.

Peer pressure and popularity

Perhaps the biggest reason bystanders turn away from victims is that they are afraid to stand out from the crowd. During adolescence, young people crave approval from their peers even more than their family. Sometimes teenagers are so eager for acceptance that they do not want to risk going against the crowd or associating with someone who is being picked on.

There is safety in numbers, which is why young people like to be a part of a group or **clique**. However, many groups have unwritten rules: everyone must dress or act a certain way to be accepted. This can include bullying or laughing when other members of the popular group do it, even if it goes against an individual's own values or feelings of empathy. If the "in" crowd says that shoving and spitting and spreading lies is all right, a teenager might go along with it, even if he or she knows it is wrong and would never do it on his or her own.

Some recent studies show that popularity is overrated, anyway. Many of those who are seen as being in the "popular" crowd are not necessarily well-liked. There are always a number of people who are popular for being kind, friendly, and trustworthy. There are also plenty who are regarded by their peers as arrogant and stuck-up. They may be envied, but they are also feared because they maintain their social position by gossiping, taunting, and excluding others.

To fit in, teenagers often dress and act like other teenagers they admire, even if it means engaging in unkind or abusive behavior.

Standing up to the crowd

Those who laugh or turn away from victims just to fit in or get someone's approval are not being themselves and probably do not like themselves much afterward. It is normal to want to do what others are doing. If this is something wrong or cruel, however, it takes courage to step out from the crowd.

Being yourself is easier said than done. It is important to figure out what you believe in, what you are good at, and what makes you feel happy and confident. Then do those things. Real friends will like the real you.

Studies have shown that young people do not need to be popular to be happy. Psychologist Kathleen McElhaney says, "Popularity isn't all that important. The key is finding a group of people with whom you can feel at ease being yourself."

EMILY'S STORY: THE POWER OF BYSTANDERS

In the book *Mean Chicks, Cliques, and Dirty Tricks*, Emily, 18, recounts the story of a girl she went to school with, who was overweight and wore the "wrong" clothes. The popular girls did everything they could to make her life miserable. They made fun of her to her face, moved from her lunch table when she sat down, and spread rumors that she had a nasty disease. When the girl developed a speech problem, the bullies made fun of that, too. Emily and her friends imagined how hard it must be for the girl to wake up every morning, knowing the torment she would face. So, she and two friends went out of their way to be kind to the girl. Six years later, Emily is still friends with the girl, who is happier now. It would have been easier for Emily to ignore her, or even join the bullies in taunting her. Instead, Emily and her friends reached out and made a positive difference in her life.

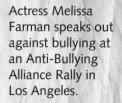

Actress Melissa Farman speaks out against bullying at an Anti-Bullying Alliance Rally in Los Angeles.

Effects of standing by

Bystanders who remain quiet in the face of abuse silently encourage bullies. Standing by also hurts more than just the victims of bullying. It can also harm the bystanders themselves. Even witnessing the violence of bullying can be traumatic. It often makes bystanders feel anxious or afraid. After all, they could be next! Sometimes, bystanders laugh at bullying only because they feel uncomfortable. If they turn away, they may feel guilty. They could also lose respect for themselves and confidence in their ability to deal with future confrontations.

Stand up, don't stand by

When bystanders are willing to say no to bullies, they can stop the bullying about half of the time. This is how to do it:

- *Take stock*: Often, bystanders are not even aware that they are participating in bullying. So, when you find yourself in a social setting, take a few moments to consider: Are the people in your group putting other people down? Are you shunning someone you do not think is popular enough? Could your words or actions be hurting someone? If your answer is yes, it may be time to change your behavior.

- *Tell the person who is bullying to stop—if you feel safe*: If you see a physical attack, write down the details of the confrontation, then hand your report to a trusted adult.

- *Reach out to bullied kids or teenagers*: Listen to their concerns. Include them in your group. Support them while they are bullied or afterward, in private.

- *Apologize*: If you do hurt someone, always apologize. Even if the victim has moved on, he or she almost certainly has not forgotten about the bullying incident. An apology can make a huge difference in a victim's life, at any age. Just hearing a bully or bystander say that the victim did not deserve such treatment can help restore the person's self-esteem. It can also help to ease your own guilt.

- *Think about it*: If you are unkind to someone, ask yourself: How did it make you feel about yourself? Why did you do or say what you did? What could you have done differently, and what could you do differently in the future?

BULLY-PREVENTION: AN ANTI-BULLYING TOOL KIT

Hermione, from the Harry Potter movies, is standing up to the bully Draco Malfoy in the movie *Harry Potter and the Prisoner of Azkaban* (2004).

MICHAEL'S STORY: USING ASSERTIVENESS TO STAND UP TO BULLIES

In her book about bullying, author Barbara Coloroso shares the story of Michael, a well-known television host who was bullied as a child. Every day, a child named Gorman demanded money from Michael. Michael would run home and steal money from his mother's purse to give to Gorman. One day, Michael felt so guilty about taking his mother's money that he told his father. He helped Michael rehearse a line to tell Gorman. The next day, when Gorman demanded money, Michael looked Gorman directly in the eye. Then he said firmly, "It's over, Gorman. There will be no more money." It *was* over. Gorman never bothered him again.

Have you heard lots of conflicting messages about how to deal with bullies? Perhaps you have been told to "just ignore" the bully or to fight back. However, most experts and victims agree that ignoring a bully does not make the problem go away. Often, this just makes the bully try harder to get a reaction, especially when he or she knows the target is unlikely to fight back. When a target repeatedly walks away from the bully, he or she is more likely to feel fearful and helpless when confronted with similar situations in the future.

On the other hand, returning an insult or a punch is not the answer, either. Since bullying involves an imbalance in power, the bully usually wins confrontations. What experts recommend is behaving neither passively nor aggressively—but rather assertively. Being assertive means telling someone exactly what you want directly, honestly, and respectfully. Assertiveness allows you to solve problems without fighting and without walking away.

It may be hard at first, but assertiveness is a skill that can be practiced and, like a muscle that is used over and over, it eventually becomes automatic. All relationships in life require a certain degree of assertiveness, so it is a good skill to learn!

Building assertiveness and self-esteem

Here are some tips on how you can stand up to the "Gormans" in your life:

- *Act with confidence*: The key word is "act." Even if you do not feel confident, keep your head up high. Know that your words account for only 7 percent of all communication. About 58 percent is body language, and 38 percent is the tone of your voice. Do not stand with your shoulders slumped, gaze at the floor, or speak in a timid voice. Do stand tall, look straight at the bullies, and speak firmly and directly, without showing fear or emotion. At first, they may be nastier because you are taking away their power. Soon, however, they will respect you.

- *Use humor*: Humor could surprise your bully enough to stop him or her. For instance, if a bully makes fun of your appearance, you could respond by saying, "Well, it's a good thing I'm not planning to go into modeling," or "Yeah, this is the new look!"

- *Assert yourself one-on-one with your bully, when others are not around*: Without an audience to impress, your bully may not be so brave. However, remember to always keep a safe physical distance from your bully.

- *Have several well-rehearsed scripts ready*: If you know, for example, that the bully will block your entrance to the cafeteria, practice saying, "Excuse me," in a calm, confident way. If you know your bully is going to insult you, you could practice saying, "I'm sorry you're having a bad day." If your bully continues to give you a hard time, continue to speak with maturity and confidence.

- *Turn the insult into a compliment*: When called "fatty," say, "Big is beautiful. Thank you." When called a "geek," say, "Thanks, I love it when people call me smart."

- *Whatever*: Respond to a bully's insults with comments like: "Whatever" or "Who cares?" in a neutral (not nasty) tone. Just make sure you are not cruel, or you will make your bully angrier.

Developing self-esteem and self-confidence are also important, because confident people are harder to bully. Here are some suggestions for raising self-esteem:

- Self-esteem literally means holding yourself in high regard. Discover and develop your unique strengths. These are the things you are naturally drawn to, even if your parents do not encourage them. Perhaps it is drawing rather than soccer, or drama instead of choir. Try joining a club in a different area. New friendships and skills will make you feel more confident, and young people with common interests often become lifelong friends.

- Direct your talents into something productive. One girl was taunted because she dressed differently from everyone else. It turned out that she made her own clothes and had an incredible eye for style. She volunteered to make costumes for the school play, where people appreciated her unique talents.

- If you want to change or improve something about yourself, then make a plan to do it.

- Exercise! Physical activity releases hormones called endorphins that help you feel good and manage stress. Exercise also helps you maintain a healthy body weight, which can improve your self-image.

Young people with good eye contact and a strong, confident posture are less likely to be targeted by bullies.

Reporting bullying

Reporting bullies helps both victims and bullies. Unfortunately, only about one-third of victims and bystanders report bullying to an adult. Why do the majority of young people stay silent?

Some are afraid the bully will retaliate if they report them. However, there is a difference between tattling and telling. If someone "tattles," he or she is usually trying to get another person in trouble. For example, a tattletale might say, "Charlie just cheated on his test." Telling, on the other hand, is a way to help get someone out of trouble. For instance, you might tell a teacher, "Charlie is punching Ashley. Ashley is crying and needs help." This could rescue Ashley from a bad situation.

Other kids are ashamed to admit they have been bullied. They need to know that there is absolutely nothing wrong with them—the problem is with the bully. Finally, some young people simply do not believe adults can help. It is important to find an adult who will take your complaint seriously and keep your identity private. If an adult ever makes you feel silly or ashamed, look for another person—a relative, school counselor, or hotline worker—until you find someone who will assist and listen to you.

STUART'S STORY:
A FORMER BULLY SPEAKS OUT

In the book *Letters to a Bullied Girl*, Stuart, a former bully, describes how guilty he feels about the pain he and his friends caused a classmate they believed was ugly. She was made the victim of extreme cyberbullying. Stuart writes, "The girl we taunted didn't deserve a moment of our torment. I wish someone had educated us about bullying because we were obviously too immature or bent on experimenting with power to realize how we were hurting her." He concludes his letter with, "I commend you for speaking up and telling your mother because you not only helped yourself, but you are also helping your bullies realize their mistakes. How I wish someone had told on me."

THINK ABOUT THIS

Samantha Shaw's ears stuck out a little and her right ear folded over at the top, in what is called a lop ear. None of the children Samantha played with seemed to notice her ears, but some of her friends' parents mentioned them to her mother. To prevent future bullying, Samantha's mother decided to get her plastic surgery to pin her ears back. The surgery was successful, but it raised a big debate over whether or not plastic surgery is an appropriate solution to bullying.

Over the last decade, the number of teenagers getting plastic surgery has increased by over 30 percent, some of it as a precaution against bullying. The most common procedures are rhinoplasty (nose jobs), breast reduction or enlargement, and otoplasty (ear surgery). Some say that the benefits to a child's self-esteem make cosmetic surgery worth the risk. Others say that allowing or encouraging children to have surgery sends a message that there is something wrong with them to begin with. If adults believe children need improving or fixing, are they guilty of being bullies themselves?

Every surgery carries some risk. Furthermore, the results may not be what the young person expected, or even what they want 10 or 20 years later.

Bullying by the numbers

Bullying victims are not alone. A U.S. study reports that up to 90 percent of fourth to eighth graders have been bullied at some point. And 50 percent of these kids say that bullying is a "big problem" at school. Studies may vary, but all of them reveal that bullying is common.

These large figures show that anyone can be bullied, and there is no special reason why bullying victims are chosen. So, bullying victims should never feel ashamed of themselves for being targeted by a bully.

It gets better

If you are bullied, you want your life to get better right away. After all, school is not just a training ground for life. It is life. However, it is helpful to remember that life after school will almost certainly look very different. Things will get better. The following real-life stories are about young people who endured school bullying, only to emerge with successful and happy lives.

TOM'S STORY: OLYMPIC CHAMPION

At the age of 14, diver Tom Daley (in the center of the picture below) became the United Kingdom's youngest competitor at the 2008 Beijing Olympics. When he returned to school, however, Tom did not receive a hero's welcome. Instead, he was mocked and called "Speedo boy" and "diver boy." Tom did his best to shrug off the bullying, but it only increased. On the playing field, kids tackled and taunted him. In the classroom, they threw pens and pencils at him. Some even threatened to break his legs. It got so bad that he finally moved to another school, one for elite athletes. He also met with a psychologist, who helped Tom focus on his positive traits. Just a month later, in July 2009, Tom became the United Kingdom's first individual world diving champion, at the age of 15. No one is bullying him now.

GEORGES'S STORY: SELF-DEFENSE

Growing up in Quebec, Canada, Georges St. Pierre was a scrawny child with acne who preferred chess to hockey. He loved school until he was 10. Then a group of older kids began to beat him up and take his clothes and money. Georges lay awake each night, planning escape routes in his head. He began taking karate, and as his martial arts skills improved, Georges became strong enough to defend himself. "By 14, 15, nobody could touch me," he says.

Now, Georges is the welterweight champion of the Ultimate Fighting Championship. Georges knows that not every bullying victim will transform into a world class fighter, but he does know that things change for everyone. Georges ran into one of his former bullies at a shopping center a few years ago. When Georges nodded his head in recognition, the bully just looked down at his shoes and shuffled along.

Celebrities who have been bullied

What do pop superstar Lady Gaga and star golfer Tiger Woods have in common? Both were bullied as children. So were actors Tom Cruise, Sandra Bullock, Robert Pattinson Miley Cyrus, and Chris Colfer. Athlete Michael Phelps was bullied, too. So were "brainiacs" Albert Einstein and Microsoft founder Bill Gates.

Why have so many of the world's most famous and successful people been victims of bullying? Author Alexandra Robbins suggests that, "Many of the differences that cause a student to be excluded in school are the identical traits that others will value, love, respect, or find compelling about the person outside the school setting." Bullied kids may also be especially determined to prove themselves and prove their bullies wrong. In fact, some victims may have developed high levels of inner strength and perseverance from enduring years of bullying.

THINK ABOUT THIS

As awareness of the harmful effects of bullying increases, many governments are creating policies to combat bullying. For this book, we talked to Kevin Jennings, who was appointed by President Barack Obama to create anti-bullying programs for schools. What Jennings has to say is useful for anyone affected by bullying.

Q: If you could offer teenagers three tips for dealing with bullies, what would they be?

A: 1. If you're the one being bullied, tell an adult what's happening.

2. If you see someone getting bullied, speak up and say, "This is not cool." If it is not safe for you to do that, tell an adult. Also, find the bullied person later, and tell them you're on their side.

3. If you're being a bully, just stop it. You look like a jerk, and people are going to think you are one if you keep it up. They may pretend to be your friend, but that's only because they are afraid of you. You don't have any real friends when you're a bully—just people who pretend to be because they don't want to be your next victim.

Q: How is the government working to help solve the bullying problem?

A: President Obama held a major conference at the White House on March 10, 2011, to bring together all the nation's education leaders to make a plan to help stop bullying. We've created resources like stopbullying.gov to help people do that.

Q: What programs effectively deal with bullying? And how can schools or local governments do more to promote these?

A: There is a lot of great information at stopbullying.gov. The most important thing is to have a very clear policy that defines bullying, trains teachers on how to stop bullying, and educates students and their families about why bullying is unacceptable.

How you can help

You can help by not being a bully, by being an ally for those who are bullied, and by reporting bullies. You can also take some bigger steps:

- Try to start an anti-bullying club at your school. Some schools have programs that partner older student **mentors** with bullying victims. The mentors, who have received anti-bully training, not only provide victims with "back-up," but they also teach victims how to deal with bullies. Some schools also have bullying hotlines, where students can **anonymously** report bullying at any time.

- Contact your local elected officials and encourage them to propose anti-bullying legislation.

- Put together an assembly or a play for your school or community, to help educate students and teachers about bullying and to spread the anti-bullying message.

- Use Facebook or Twitter to organize anti-bullying rallies or campaigns in support of kids who are being bullied.

- Be a leader. Stand up for younger children who are being bullied.

These students in New York City are taking a stand by painting an anti-bullying mural at their school.

WHAT HAVE WE LEARNED?

THINK ABOUT THIS

Many schools have adopted tough "zero-tolerance" policies for bullying or violence. These policies state that any words, threats, or actions defined as "bullying" will not be tolerated under any circumstances. Anyone who disobeys is suspended or expelled. These programs sound like a good idea, and some people believe they work.

Others disagree. Some studies have shown that traditional punishments such as suspension or expulsion just puts bullies at greater risk of repeating their bad behavior, and even of committing crimes, than bullies who are paired with mentors. Bullies who are suspended often return to school angrier and more likely to take it out on vulnerable classmates.

Many also object to the "one-size-fits-all" punishments found in some zero-tolerance policies. Should a victim who fights back after repeatedly being bullied receive the same punishment as the child who has tormented him or her?

Some anti-bullying activists suggest that, instead of suspending students, schools should first examine what is happening in a bully's home life. One school discovered that a bully was stealing students' lunch money simply because he was hungry. Once the school has figured out why the bully is behaving in a certain manner, the bully could apologize to the victim and be punished appropriately. For example, if a girl teases an overweight student, she could be required to help at an eating disorder clinic. This approach would teach bullies to have more understanding of others, while also ensuring that schools have zero tolerance for bullies' harmful words and actions.

If you are being bullied, you may feel hopeless or helpless. You may believe that things will never change. Take heart: things are *already* changing. As more people become aware of the harmful effects of bullying, bullying is becoming less acceptable. Schools are establishing anti-bullying programs, and politicians are establishing anti-bullying laws and regulations.

Even if these changes have not yet reached your school, there are things you can do to fight bullying. If cyberbullies use the Internet to bully you, you can use it to find anti-bullying resources and reach out to your real friends. If cruel girls or boys spread nasty rumors about you, you can calmly and confidently confront them. If a group of bullies insults a classmate, you can let your classmate know that there is nothing wrong with him or her, only the bullies.

Australian bullying victim Casey Haynes (right) was expelled from school after picking up and throwing down a bully who repeatedly hit him. Here, he joins forces with boxing trainer Christian Marchegiani's Underdogs, an anti-bullying campaign.

Remember, the most important thing you can do is to be yourself. Once you start discovering and developing your unique personality and strengths, you will feel better about yourself. People with confidence are less likely to be bullied or feel the need to bully others. If you feel good about yourself, you will attract real friends and will not feel the need to gain the approval of anyone else—especially bullies!

RESEARCH AND DEBATE

You can find out more about bullying from a variety of sources. Think about whether your source is reliable and consider the perspective of the person who produced it. Might the person be trying to promote a particular point of view?

Books

Nonfiction books written for young people are an excellent source of accurate and accessible information. Written by professional writers and checked by experts, the materials have been designed especially for young readers and provide a balanced view of the topic, backed up by evidence. Check the publication date of the book and try to find the most up-to-date titles.

Web sites

Web sites run by highly respected, established organizations working with people who have been bullied or who are bullies are excellent sources of trustworthy information (see page 55). They usually have case studies and quotes, so you can find firsthand information about other people's experiences.

Firsthand information is also available from surveys about bullying. Organizations working with young people often publish the results of their research online. Check that the source is recent, to ensure the information is up-to-date.

A warning about sources

Not all web sites are helpful or reliable. Anyone can set up a web site or blog and write what they like; no one checks if it is true or not. Beware of sites that are run by individuals and express their point of view alone.

Chat rooms on topics such as bullying can be a great way to interact with others who have shared similar experiences. Speaking with other bystanders or victims can help you feel supported. However, it is extremely important to use chat rooms with caution.

Since chat sessions are "live," users may say things that are inappropriate or even hurtful. Also, some young people you meet there might not even actually be young. They could be adults who want to hurt young people. Make sure you never reveal personal information, such as your name or address, and never agree to meet anyone from a chat room in person.

Organize your research materials

If you are researching bullying for a school project, start by organizing your research materials into different categories. You could use the concept web below as a starting point:

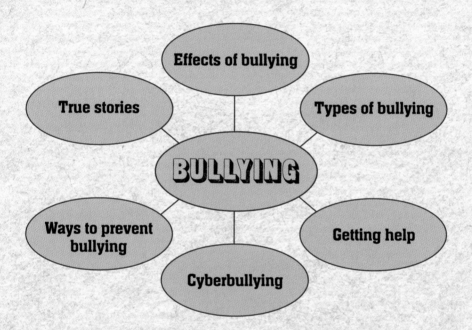

Using information for discussion and debate

If you are planning a discussion about bullying, remember that it is an extremely sensitive topic. Remember that in a class of 30 students, there are certain to be some who are being bullied or are bullies themselves. You may want to use role-playing in your debate. Different groups could adopt a different perspective on bullying and argue from that point of view. You could also use the topics in the "Think about this" boxes in this book as discussion points.

GLOSSARY

amygdala pair of brain structures involved in the processing and expression of emotions, especially anger and fear

anonymity state of being unknown or unidentified

anonymous having an unknown identity

anorexia eating disorder in which a person has an obsessive and unrealistic fear of gaining weight and refuses to maintain a healthy body weight

antisocial unwilling or unable to associate normally with other people; hostile or unfriendly toward others

assertive having or showing a confident personality

bulimia emotional disorder in which periods of extreme overeating are followed by depression and/or self-induced vomiting or fasting

bystander person who is present at an event without participating in it

clique small group of people who spend their time together and do not allow others to join them

cyberbullying using electronic technology, such as e-mail, instant messaging, web sites, or texts, to bully someone

direct bullying using words or violence to abuse someone face-to-face

domestic abuse pattern of behavior that causes physical or emotional harm to a partner in a relationship

empathize able to understand another person's feelings

empathy ability to understand another person's feelings

epileptic related to a physical condition in which there is a sudden, brief change in how the brain works, resulting in unconsciousness or seizures

frontal lobe each of the paired lobes of the brain located immediately behind the forehead, including areas that deal with behavior, learning, personality, and voluntary movement

harass continually irritate, torment, or bother someone

indirect bullying abuse that is conducted behind someone's back through gossip, shunning, or bullying those who want to associate with the victim

intimidate frighten or threaten someone so that he or she does what you want

manipulative trying to influence someone else's emotions or behavior for one's own selfish purposes

medium means by which something is communicated or accomplished

mentor experienced and trusted adviser

paralyzed temporary or permanent inability to move a part or most of the body, usually as a result of illness, poison, or injury

passive rarely initiating action; obeying without resistance

peer person who is the same age and in the same social circle as you

physical bullying using violent acts such as kicking, punching, or hitting to gain power over peers

relational aggression type of abuse in which someone tries to harm a person's relationships or social standing in a group

self-esteem feeling of being happy with your own character and abilities

sexual harassment any unwanted or uninvited sexual behavior that is offensive, embarrassing, intimidating, or humiliating, including sexually offensive language or unwanted pressure for sexual activity

target person, object, or place selected as the aim of an attack

taunt provoke a person with insulting remarks

tease provoke a person in a playful, friendly way

traumatic extremely unpleasant and causing someone to be very upset

unconscious condition similar to sleep, in which you do not see, feel, or think, usually because you are sick or injured

verbal bullying using language such as swear words or insults to intentionally harm another person

vulnerable easily hurt by criticism or rejection

FIND OUT MORE

Books

Gardner, Olivia, Emily Buder, and Sarah Buder. *Letters to a Bullied Girl: Messages of Healing and Hope.* New York: HarperCollins, 2008.

Guillain, Charlotte. *Coping with Bullying* (Real Life Issues). Chicago: Heinemann Library, 2011.

Jacobs, Thomas A. *Teen Cyberbullying Investigated: Where Do Your Rights End and Consequences Begin?* Minneapolis: Free Spirit, 2010.

Jakubiak, David J. *A Smart Kid's Guide to Online Bullying.* New York: PowerKids, 2010.

Kowalski, Robin M., Susan P. Limber, and Patricia W. Agatston. *Cyberbullying: Bullying in the Digital Age.* Malden, Mass.: Wiley-Blackwell, 2012.

Ludwig, Trudy, and Beth Adams. *Confessions of a Former Bully.* Berkeley, Calif.: Tricycle, 2010.

Miller, Michaela. *Stories About Surviving Gangs and Bullying* (Real Life Heroes). Mankato, Minn.: Arcturus, 2010.

Shearin Karres, Erika. *Mean Chicks, Cliques, and Dirty Tricks: A Real Girl's Guide to Getting Through It All.* Avon, Mass.: Adams Media, 2010.

Winkler, Kathleen. *Bullying: How to Deal with Taunting, Teasing, and Tormenting* (Issues in Focus Today). Berkeley Heights, N.J.: Enslow, 2005.

Web sites

www.bullying.org
This interactive web site is dedicated to raising awareness about bullying. Bullying victims can both learn from and share their stories with others.

www.itgetsbetter.org
The "It Gets Better Project" is dedicated to showing gay teens that the difficulties they might face—such as bullying—will get better for them in the future. Many people share their personal stories on this web site.

www.pbs.org/inthemix/bullying/
"Stop Bullying ... Take a Stand!" is a 30-minute documentary for teens about bullying, developed as part of an award-winning Public Broadcasting Service teen series.

www.stopbullying.gov
This government web site offers resources on bullying for kids, teens, parents, and educators, including webisodes about taking a stand on bullying, a list of warning signs, ways to get help, and information about cyberbullying.

survivingbullies.com
This web site offers information and resources, including informational videos, about bullying.

Topics to debate

- Can or should bullies be held responsible for the emotional harm and suicides they cause?
- Are some young people hardwired to be bullies? A study suggests that about 5 percent of children suffer from "aggressive conduct disorder." When these children see violence, the "reward" or "pleasure" centers of their brains light up.
- Will bullying continue as long as we live in a competitive society?
- Are people becoming less empathetic? A study suggests that young people are far less empathetic now than they were 30 years ago. Does technology play a role in distancing people from each other?

INDEX